The Chamique Holdsclaw Story

BY KRISTI NELSON

SCHOLASTIC INC.
New York   Toronto   London   Auckland   Sydney
Mexico City   New Delhi   Hong Kong

To my parents, Gene and Helen Nelson

PHOTO CREDITS
NBA Photos
Cover, 8, 65: Mitchell Layton. **Cover (Inset Photo), 6:** Glenn James.
Back Cover: Ray Amati. **15, 23, 26:** Bob Mackey.
31, 33, 36, 41, 46, 49, 53: Brian Spurlock.
59, 69, 72: Andrew D. Bernstein **60:** David Liam Kyle.

PHOTO CREDITS: INSERT SECTION
NBA Photos
I: Charles Smith. **II, V, VI:** Mitchell Layton. **III:** Fernando Medina.
IV: David Liam Kyle. **II, V, VI:** Glenn James.

If you purchased this book without a cover, you should be aware that this book is stolen property. It was reported as "unsold and destroyed" to the publisher, and neither the author nor the publisher has received any payment for this "stripped book."

No part of this work may be reproduced, stored in a retrieval system, or transmitted in any form or by any means, electronic, mechanical, photocopying, recording, or otherwise, without written permission of the publisher. For information regarding permission, write to Scholastic Inc., Attention: Permissions Department, 555 Broadway, New York, NY 10012.

The WNBA and individual WNBA team identifications, photographs and other content used on or in this publication are trademarks, copyrighted designs and other forms of intellectual property of WNBA Enterprises, LLC and may not be used, in whole or in part, without the prior written consent of WNBA Enterprises, LLC. All rights reserved.

ISBN 0-439-16948-8

Copyright © 2000 by WNBA Enterprises, LLC
All rights reserved. Published by Scholastic Inc.

SCHOLASTIC and associated logos are trademarks and/or registered trademarks of Scholastic Inc.

12 11 10 9 8 7 6 5 4 3 2 1   0 1 2 3 4 5 6/0

Printed in the U.S.A.
First Scholastic printing, April 2000
Book Design: Michael Malone

TABLE OF CONTENTS

Introduction: The New Millennium..................6

1. Growing Up in the Big City....................10

2. A Basketball Star Is Born......................14

3. High School Hero...................................22

4. Welcome to Tennessee!........................30

5. Not a Freshman Anymore.....................40

6. Senior Year Lessons..............................48

7. Welcome to the WNBA..........................58

8. Let the Games Begin!...........................64

Career Highlights.......................................78

INTRODUCTION

THE NEW MILLENNIUM

It was the evening of the USA Basketball team's opening game at the 1999 U.S. Olympic Cup games. The team's youngest player, Chamique Holdsclaw, was preparing to run onto the court and take big steps toward reaching another of her goals.

When the time came, Chamique hopped off the bench, jogged onto the court, and immediately drilled a 15-foot baseline jumper. She then grabbed an offensive rebound and put that in the basket, too. Later in the game, she converted a turnover into a layup.

INTRODUCTION

By the end of the game, Team USA had won, 86–67, and Chamique, who scored 11 points, was one of five players on the American team to score in double figures. It was another good game for the young basketball superstar.

Just a few weeks before, Chamique had wrapped up her first WNBA season with a Rookie of the Year Award and a vote to the All-WNBA Second Team. Now, in the U.S. Olympic Cup games, Chamique had the rare opportunity to represent the 1999–2000 USA Women's team on its way to the 2000 Olympic Games in Sydney, Australia.

After just one professional season, Chamique Holdsclaw has proven to be one of the most popular and exciting players in the WNBA. She is already one of the most celebrated women's basketball players of all time and will only get better. She inspires a new generation of female basketball players with her grace and ability, and has dazzled basketball fans since she was in high school.

Lisa Leslie, a fellow WNBA player and Chamique's USA teammate, has said that Chamique is the player who will take women's basketball to the next level. "Chamique is going to be the player for the next millennium," Leslie told *The Washington Post*. "She's really going to open the doors for all of us."

Chamique entered the WNBA after a highly successful college career. She arrived accompanied by a lot of hype and had to prove herself in the pros. But

INTRODUCTION

Chamique dazzles fans during her first season in the WNBA as a star player for the Washington Mystics.

INTRODUCTION

in a very short time, Chamique has earned the respect of her teammates and WNBA fans everywhere. Everyone has something positive to say about her.

"What she means can't be measured," said track star Jackie Joyner-Kersee, who is one of the best female athletes in the world. "She has changed the face of women's sports. She has brought ordinary people into watching the sport."

Chamique's first professional coach, Nancy Darsch of the Washington Mystics, said, "She definitely has a very, very bright future. She is and will be a great player."

As Tennessee Lady Vols Coach Pat Summitt once said, "There's only one Chamique," and despite all the attention she gets, Chamique doesn't feel pressure to do anything but become a better player and continue to be true to herself.

"I know what I'm capable of doing," Chamique has said. "I know if I work hard, I know great things will happen. I know what got me here, and I'm humble. It's cool to have things [like shoe contracts and other endorsements], it shows how women's sports have grown, and I'm opening doors for others coming behind me."

CHAPTER 1

Growing Up in the Big City

Ask anyone at the Astoria Houses in Queens, New York, about Chamique Holdsclaw and you would likely hear a mini-biography. Everyone knows how Chamique used to play basketball for hours every day until her grandmother, June, would yell out the window for her to come in for dinner. And many people could probably even point out the apartment where Chamique grew up from age 11 on—an apartment with a kitchen-window view of the basketball court. But before she was known as a famous basketball superstar, Chamique Shaunta Holdsclaw was just a girl practicing basketball on her neighborhood courts in Queens, New York.

Chamique was born on August 9, 1977, in Flushing, Queens. As a child, Chamique was friendly and polite but very, very shy. She would often get nervous around strangers and wouldn't talk to just anyone. It seemed that she had built a wall around herself to keep people from getting in. "She talked with her eyes," her grandmother, June Holdsclaw, explained. "She never said much."

Although she was shy, there were a few people who knew how to find the real Chamique. June, whom Chamique adored, was one of them. She was also very close to her younger brother, Davon. With the two of them she would laugh and joke around, but basketball usually helped bring out her personality when she was around other people.

Chamique enjoyed playing a lot of sports, but she developed an attachment to basketball when she was very young. Part of the reason is that her grandmother had played on sandlots as a youngster in Alabama, and had passed her fondness for the game on to her granddaughter. Chamique also learned a lot about basketball from one of her uncles, who would let young Chamique follow him onto the court.

Chamique's true start as a basketball player came at about age five or six when she and Davon got into the habit of playing basketball inside. They would hang a wire clothes hanger over a door to make a basketball hoop and would use a rolled-up pair of sweat socks as a ball.

THE FACTS OF LIFE
Born: 8/9/1977
Height: 6-2
Weight: 167

When they visited their grandmother at the Astoria Houses, they would play sweat-sock basketball for hours in her hallway. For the adults, including their parents Benita Holdsclaw and Willie Johnson, it was sometimes very annoying. "She went through so many hangers," June said. "All I would hear is bump, bump, bump."

Today, Chamique is probably one of the most famous former residents of the Astoria Houses, a sprawling housing project of high-rise buildings along the East River in Astoria, Queens. Chamique and her brother Davon went to live there with their grandmother in 1988 after their parents broke up. Chamique was 11 years old and Davon was eight. June, who worked as a hospital records clerk, was able to give the kids a stable home and a structured environment. She instilled the values of education and religion into her young grandchildren.

Living with her grandmother was tough at first. Chamique had always been close to her dad, and living without him was sometimes depressing. But she soon adapted to her grandmother's strict rules and was more comfortable in her new home. She and Davon knew they had to do their homework as soon as they came home from school and were required to attend church every Sunday.

June also made sure her grandchildren were always busy. "On Saturdays, you're not going to be hanging around in the streets doing nothing," she told Chamique. So Chamique spent much of her time at the Boys and Girls Club or at church doing arts and crafts.

Although June lived only a few minutes away from where Chamique had lived with her parents, she was separated from her old friends and found herself in a new neighborhood full of unfamiliar faces.

During that first summer at her grandmother's apartment, Chamique spent most of her time hanging out with a couple of older kids who were friends of the family. One of them, Andrew, went to the playground to play basketball every day. Chamique would tag along and watch the older boys run up and down the courts for hours.

When the boys finished their games, Chamique would shoot and play by herself, or play one-on-one with Andrew. Eventually, the group of boys started to notice

GROWING UP IN THE BIG CITY

how good she was and would let her play with them. Pretty soon, she was accepted as one of the guys.

Even though her game was already pretty good, Chamique didn't dream of becoming a professional basketball player in those days. In fact, she wanted to be a lawyer. Her favorite subjects in school were history and Spanish, and she liked visiting the homes of her Spanish-speaking friends to try to understand what everyone was saying.

There was also a short time when Chamique took ballet lessons, and even performed in a recital at New York City's Lincoln Center. But ballet fell by the wayside as Chamique spent more and more time playing basketball, not thinking that someday she would be playing professionally alongside some of the greatest women basketball players in the world.

Chamique learned and improved her basketball skills by competing with boys from her neighborhood on playground courts. "I was just out there every day playing with the guys," Chamique remembered. "When I got pushed down, it was kind of like I had to get right back up. I couldn't complain and I couldn't cry, because if I did, they wouldn't let me play the next day."

CHAMIQUE'S FAVORITES
Recording Artists: Brandy, Monica and Whitney Houston
Foods: Pork chops, corn and collard greens
Ice Cream: Pistachio
Athletes: Michael Jordan, Scottie Pippen and Teresa Edwards

CHAPTER 2

A Basketball Star Is Born

Chamique was 11 when she finally tried out for an organized basketball team—an all-boys recreation team in the Police Athletic League. Although Chamique loved the game, she was too timid to ask to join and was often intimidated by the boys on the team. Grandma June had to step in on her behalf.

"I would be outside all the time playing, I just didn't make the effort to try to join any teams," Chamique said. "I was kind of shy, so my grandmother went out there and told the coach that she wanted me to play."

June didn't know how good Chamique was yet, she just knew that her granddaughter liked to play the game, and she wanted to make sure that she was happy. "You could always see Chamique on the basketball court, shooting and jumping around all the time," June said. "That's the way she spent her spare time."

At first, things were tough for Chamique on the boy's basketball team. She struggled to fit in and get along with her teammates. But she adapted quickly to them, and they to her.

When Chamique was a freshman on the varsity team at Christ the King High School, no one knew how great she would become.

"It was fun," she remembered. "The first year I went, they kind of didn't want a girl on their team, but then the second year I tried out and I was the best player on the team. So I went from not being wanted to being one of the best."

But the playground was a slightly different story. Chamique often played against boys who were older than she was. When she was 11 or 12 years old, she would sometimes play with boys who were as old as 14 or 15. When she first started playing with the guys on the playground, she was horrible compared to them.

"Nobody wanted to pick me," she explained. So she started to practice, usually six to eight hours a day, before and after school. As soon her final class was over, Chamique would head straight home to play basketball. Her classmates called her "flat leaver," because she would just "flat leave" to play basketball after school.

"Sometimes I'd get up and play at seven in the morning, and then when I'd get out of school, I'd play again, from two-thirty to, like, eight or nine at night."

Even the weather could not stop Chamique from playing basketball. She would play in the rain, and if it snowed, she would go out and shovel off the court so she could still practice. June Holdsclaw's kitchen window looks out over the basketball court at the Astoria Houses

> **BIGGEST WISH**
> What is the one thing that Chamique would most like to change about herself? "Do away with my shyness."

where Chamique used to spend much of her time. June would often look out and watch Chamique play. She played so much that sometimes she wouldn't remember to go home to eat, and June often had to yell out the window to make Chamique come inside.

"If she was playing with the boys and it was getting

> She would play in the rain, and if it snowed, she would go out and shovel off the court so she could still practice.

to, like, eight or nine o'clock, I would yell out the window, 'Chamique! Come in for dinner!'" June explained. The calls embarrassed Chamique, who would hiss, "Grandma, don't do that!" But if June hadn't called her in, Chamique might have played basketball all night. The boys usually wanted to play game after game until they could finally beat her.

"And then when I lost to the guys, I didn't want to go up," she said. "I just wanted to keep playing."

Although Chamique and her little brother, Davon, were very close, she would often have to drag him with her to games. "Do we have to go?" Davon would ask. "I don't want to go."

The other boys would tease Davon on the playground and say, "Man, your sister is good!"

Chamique was a good kid, and usually did as her grandmother asked. But sometimes she displayed a rebellious streak. When she was 12, Chamique skipped school

THE CHAMIQUE HOLDSCLAW STORY

> **ADDICTED TO FUN**
> Chamique considers herself "an arcade freak." She loves her PlayStation, NFL Blitz, and takes her computer with her everywhere. She has also been known to order ten movies at one time and says she could sit home all day watching movies.

for three days to shoot baskets by herself on the Astoria Houses' court. Of course, June was very angry about her missing school and punished Chamique.

June also enforced the rule that if Chamique didn't get up for church, she couldn't play basketball on Sundays. But one Sunday, Chamique decided to skip church and head to the playground for a game or two. She was still out there when her grandmother returned from services. Chamique was grounded for two weeks.

Chamique gives her grandmother a lot of credit for her basketball career, for school, and for keeping her on the straight path. "I just thank God for my grandmother because she definitely implemented structure in my life," she said. "I thought that was key, because I could have been out there running every which direction, but it's like she set a path for me and I followed that path. At the time, I was kind of rebellious and didn't want to do the things that she insisted I do. But I realize now that everything did pay off."

After Chamique led her rec league team in scoring, everyone wanted her on their teams. They liked her because she was a good shooter and because she was tall,

A BASKETBALL STAR IS BORN

oftentimes taller than the boys her age. Chamique started to travel with her friends from the neighborhood to basketball courts around the city in search of competitive pickup games.

"Early in the morning we would meet. We would say 'We're going to go to Astoria Park,' or 'We're going to go uptown to play.' It was like an adventure. We would go everywhere and play. I don't even remember some of the places I played, I would just go with my friends. It was cool."

One of the guys she used to play pickup games with was Ron Artest, the former St. John's star who was a first-round pick in the 1999 NBA Draft. Chamique grew up just eight blocks away from Artest. He was little and "kind of dorky then," Chamique said, so she was always chosen ahead of him.

"She inspired me to be good," Artest told *Newsday*. "When she was in junior high, we always said she would be the best. I look up to her now. I wouldn't even want to play her now. I respect her too much to even step on the court with her. She is the king in New York."

Chamique's playground experiences made her a tougher player, because the boys played a very physical game. She developed her outside shot because she knew that she couldn't risk injury against the bigger boys on the inside. Some of the flair and creativity that are now a noticeable part of Chamique's game came from years of practice on the playground. She picked up her crossover dribble there, and because having your shot blocked on the playground is the ultimate embarrassment, she learned to shoot from all over the court. Back then, she

THE CHAMIQUE HOLDSCLAW STORY

By the time Chamique finished eighth grade, a buzz was already being generated around the neighborhood and on the playgrounds about the girl from the Astoria Houses.

often had to come up with some wise shots and fancy moves to outsmart the other team. Sometimes, she'd go up to make a shot, but would decide to change it at the last second.

Playground matches also helped Chamique set goals for herself because she always wanted to beat the player who shot or dribbled better. She picked up her desire to win on the playground. Winning was very important to players on the inner-city courts because if they lost the game, they would lose the court they were playing on. Chamique was no exception. Those lessons have carried over into her adult life and affect her attitude in today's WNBA games.

In the eighth grade, Chamique was about 5-10, taller than most kids her age. Other kids would call her "Bony," or any other name that would describe a person as skinny with big feet. But Chamique didn't get upset about the name-calling. Instead, she would laugh about it and make fun of them!

It was around then that Chamique learned one of her most important lessons from June, one that she is reminded of every day—whenever she looks at her jersey.

A BASKETBALL STAR IS BORN

June explained how Chamique chose the jersey number that would be hers for years to come. "She said, 'I can have number 23, like Michael Jordan,'" June recalled. "I said 'No, Chamique, you're going to use number 23 because it represents the 23rd Psalm, the one that begins, "The Lord is my shepherd, I shall not want."' And I repeated it to her and she said, 'All right, Grandma.' But at that time, we had no idea that she was going to make the team!" But Chamique did make the team, and she has kept number 23 ever since.

By the time Chamique finished eighth grade, a buzz was already being generated around the neighborhood and on the playgrounds about the girl from the Astoria Houses. Her eighth-grade team won their championship, thanks in large part to Chamique, but neither Chamique nor her family thought that she would someday be a star.

"We just knew she was a good basketball player," June said. "It kept her busy. I never thought that it was going to come to all of this."

CHAPTER 3

High School Hero

Vincent Cannizzaro distinctly remembers the first time he saw Chamique Holdsclaw play basketball. Cannizzaro, the basketball coach at Christ the King High School in Queens, New York, had heard about Chamique from a friend. The friend told Cannizzaro he should come out to a park in Astoria one Saturday morning and watch Chamique play.

Chamique was doing some drills with a boys' team in the park when Cannizzaro arrived. He watched as she took a pass, jumped and shot the ball right over a defender. Cannizzaro, who hadn't even walked into the park yet, decided to go home.

"Don't you want to go in and see them play?" his friend asked.

"No, I've seen enough," Cannizzaro replied as he walked away, impressed by what he had seen.

Less than a year later, Chamique was on Christ the King's varsity girls' squad—the only freshman on the team. Although she only started in one game that first year, it didn't take long for Chamique to make her mark at Christ the King, a school that has one of the best basketball programs in the nation. Whenever she had a

By her sophomore year in high school, Chamique had become a true star—some members of the boys' basketball team would stick around after their own practice to watch her play.

chance to play in a game, she made an impact.

The summer after her freshman year in high school, Chamique wanted to play with her older varsity teammates on an Amateur Athletic Union (AAU) squad. Cannizzaro convinced Chamique to play with her own age group, on a 14-and-under AAU team. It was then that a light went on in Chamique's head.

"I guess I kind of dominated the 14-and-under AAU bracket," she said. "And that's when I realized that I was kind of better than everyone my age."

During her next season at Christ the King, Chamique improved dramatically. She hadn't gotten the chance to play during much of her freshman year, but in her sophomore season, she became a star.

> **Although she was an All-America player, Chamique worked very hard, sometimes harder than everyone else.**

It wasn't long before members of the boys' basketball team would remain after their own practice just to watch Chamique play. One radio broadcaster who saw Chamique in a game could only stammer, "She-she-she plays like a guy."

Chamique even impressed long-time University of Tennessee women's basketball Coach Pat Summitt, who first saw Chamique play at an AAU tournament in Chattanooga, Tennessee. Summitt had seen a lot of great basketball players in her time, but in her opinion,

HIGH SCHOOL HERO

Chamique was one of the best. Summitt continued to follow Chamique's performance throughout the rest of her high school career.

Cannizzaro had told his star player that she could revolutionize the women's game because of the way she played, but only if she set her mind to it.

"I think that you can be a great player," Cannizzaro told her. "Maybe the best that has ever played."

His belief in her made Chamique go out and work even harder.

More and more people were now watching her. At every game, Chamique was proving herself a fan favorite. At one game during her junior year, the team played a game in Altoona, Pennsylvania, against a team ranked among the top five teams in the country. In a packed gym, Chamique came out and hit her first 12 shots. When she missed the 13th shot, the entire audience stood up and applauded her anyway—not for missing the shot, but for hitting the first 12.

Although she was an All-America player, Chamique worked very hard, sometimes harder than everyone else.

"I put so much time into basketball, almost ten months a year," she said. "What am I going to get out of it if I don't work hard?"

Everyone wanted to talk to Chamique about basketball, which she sometimes found frustrating.

"I hate it when the only thing people talk to me about is basketball," she said. "Basketball sometimes gets annoying." She had other interests, like watching TV or hanging out at her friends' houses. Through it all, Chamique managed to remain a good student, with a solid B-average.

THE CHAMIQUE HOLDSCLAW STORY

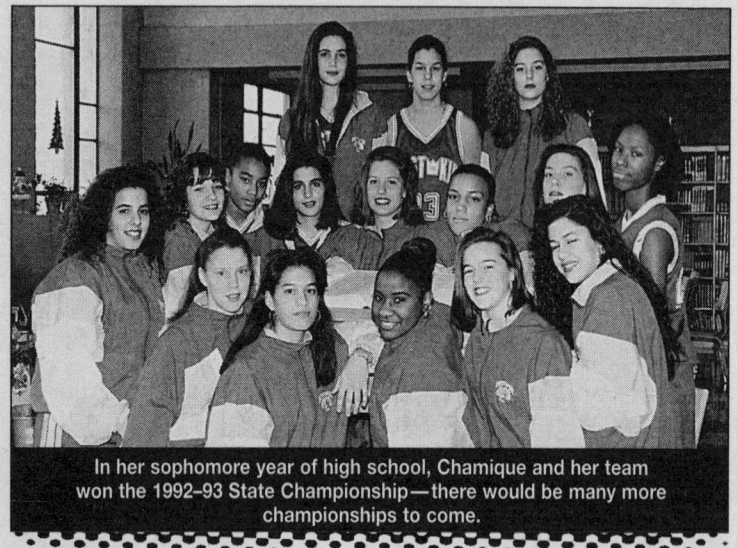

In her sophomore year of high school, Chamique and her team won the 1992–93 State Championship—there would be many more championships to come.

She would come home from practice at around 9 P.M. and immediately hit the books to study and prepare for tests in classes like art, religion, chemistry, math or Spanish.

Chamique also loved to shop and would spend hours at the mall if she could get away with it. She never really bothered with designer labels, but her clothes always matched and were perfectly pressed.

"She was perfect," said one former Christ the King teammate.

She especially liked to watch other people play basketball, in the games going on around town. "In New York, it's very competitive and there was always a game going on somewhere, with guys like Stephon Marbury and Felipe Lopez," Chamique said. "So many great players."

One problem that Chamique had throughout her successful high school seasons was getting pumped up to play teams that she knew Christ the King could beat easily. Her coaches would get angry with her for not playing to her full potential. At one such game, Chamique scored 24 points to help Christ the King win by more than 50 points. Cannizzaro and his staff chastised Chamique for not taking the game seriously enough.

As Chamique got older, she started to think more about where she wanted to go to college. Hundreds of colleges from across the

> **Hundreds of colleges from across the country were sending her letters, and coaches from big universities with impressive programs would show up at Christ the King practices or games to watch her play.**

country were sending her letters, and coaches from big universities with impressive programs would show up at Christ the King practices or games to watch her play. There were some weeks when Chamique would spot a different college coach in the gym every day.

"It's really strange to have someone always watching you," Chamique wrote in a diary she prepared for *USA Today* during her junior year of high school. "Sometimes I wonder what they are actually looking for. They leave you little notes after the game. I have a few. They say

THE CHAMIQUE HOLDSCLAW STORY

> **SUCCESS x FOUR**
> Chamique led Christ the King High School to four consecutive state championships and one national title. When she graduated, the team had an overall record of 106–4.

they hope I'm interested in their program."

Many people suggested that the New York prodigy attend school closer to home, like at the University of Connecticut. But Chamique was interested in the University of Tennessee and Tennessee Coach Pat Summitt, one of women's basketball's best-known and most-celebrated coaches. And Summitt still had her eye on Chamique. Any time Summitt would show up in the gym, it seemed that Chamique would start playing a little bit harder.

Chamique also knew she wanted to play in front of large crowds. "People in other states are more crazy about women's basketball" than in New York, she said. She knew that the Tennessee Lady Vols had a large following.

When trying to convince Chamique to go to school at Tennessee, Summitt never promised her she would be a star. Instead, Summitt impressed Chamique simply by telling her that if she worked hard, she could help the program. Summitt said there would be a lot of fierce competition, but Chamique could come out on top with hard work.

"When she said, 'I will help you become the best player possible,' that turned my head," Chamique said.

In the four years Chamique spent at Christ the King,

the school won four state titles, was ranked in the top three nationally each year, and lost only four games. She could only hope her college career would be as successful. Chamique finished high school with more than 2,000 career points and was a three-time prep All-American. She received a number of honors, including being named New York City's Player of the Year three consecutive years, the first player—male or female—to do so.

Chamique's high school success was certainly a sign of things to come.

CHAPTER 4

Welcome to Tennessee!

Chamique became the 100th player to commit to play for Coach Pat Summitt at the University of Tennessee, and she arrived with a reputation. She was one of the most highly publicized freshmen to ever play in the women's college game. She was constantly being compared to basketball pioneers Lynette Woodard, a four-time All-American athlete and the first woman to play for the Harlem Globetrotters, and Cheryl Miller, a member of the Naismith Memorial Basketball Hall of Fame who helped the U.S. women's Olympic team win their first gold in 1984. All this attention made the normally shy girl a little nervous.

> **HOME SWEET HOME**
> When Chamique left New York to go to school in Tennessee, she wasn't homesick because she had done a lot of traveling before she went to college. But she did miss New York-style pizza and shopping in New York, because that was her way to relax.

Chamique arrived at Tennessee not sure of what to expect.

THE CHAMIQUE HOLDSCLAW STORY

Coach Summitt was among the people who thought Chamique's style was a lot like Miller's. While recruiting Chamique, Summitt would often tell her so. But Chamique didn't want to be like anyone else. "She kept telling me, 'I don't want to be Cheryl Miller,'" Summitt remembered. "'I want to be Chamique Holdsclaw.'"

> From the beginning, Summitt told Chamique that at Tennessee she would become one of the best basketball players in the country.

Things were very different for Chamique when she arrived at Tennessee. She was far from home and suffered from a little culture shock in Knoxville, which was not at all like New York City. She missed her favorite New York-style pizza and the abundant shopping in New York. Adjusting to a southern town with shorter buildings and farmland was a little bit more difficult than Chamique had imagined, and she had to adjust to a new coach—who was known for being intense—and a very demanding basketball program.

From the beginning, Summitt told Chamique that at Tennessee she would become one of the best basketball players in the country. "I'm going to work you," she told Chamique. "You want to be the best player, you're going to have to work for it."

During her first few weeks, Chamique felt she couldn't keep up with the workouts. At Christ the King she hadn't

WELCOME TO TENNESSEE!

Chamique jumps over her opponent and to the hoop in a game against the University of Georgia.

had to do much to stay on top, but at Tennessee, she would have to play with and against athletes who were just as good, and sometimes better, than she was. Despite her playing ability, Chamique wasn't naturally physically strong. If her coaches tried to get her to do a weight-lifting exercise, Chamique would practically fall over.

"Coach Summitt just constantly got on me, from day one when I arrived on campus," Chamique said. Summitt told Chamique that her ballhandling skills were "average," and that she was the worst rebounder to ever be in the program. On one early-morning conditioning run, Chamique got so sick that she threw up.

"Oh, this is going to be hard," she told herself that day. And as a college freshman, she was easily intimidated, too. Once, Chamique jostled Summitt during a one-on-one drill and was so flustered that she could only stammer, "I'm sorry, oh my gosh...I'm so sorry."

Chamique thought about transferring to a different school, or going back to New York. She called her grandmother, June, to ask for permission to come home.

"No, Chamique, you're not coming home," her grand-

> Summitt was pleased when, during a game against Vanderbilt, Chamique finally grabbed her coach's jacket and said, "Coach Summitt, gimme the ball!"

WELCOME TO TENNESSEE!

mother said. Besides, June was an Alabama native, and wanted Chamique to have the experience of going to a good, southern school. "You have to just work hard, and if you work hard and listen to what the coaches say and abide by the rules, you'll be all right."

So Chamique didn't give up. Eventually, she made more friends and adjusted to both Knoxville and the Tennessee program and things became a little easier. She also started to develop more confidence in herself.

"Coach Summitt always told me, 'Meek, you're going to be one of the best players to ever play this game,' and so did my high school coach. And I would sit there and think, 'Whatever. Are you sure?'"

One of the friends Chamique made was Kellie Jolly, who was also a freshman. Jolly was from Sparta, Tennessee. The two had originally met while they were on an official campus visit to the University of Tennessee. Chamique had joked, "We'll both come here and we'll win four championships."

Kellie and Chamique remained close over the years, and Chamique even visited Kellie in Sparta, where they would ride horses together. In turn, Chamique would take Kellie on shopping sprees back in New York.

Chamique had been a B- student in high school, but after her first semester at Tennessee, she had a 2.6 grade point average—barely a C+. Coach Summitt knew that Chamique could do a lot better. Summitt made Chamique go to study hall, and the next semester, Chamique's grade point average rose to a 3.75.

"She knew it was there in me," Chamique said.

Chamique called herself "square," because all she

seemed to do was play basketball and go to class. If people would wave to her on campus, she'd simply wave back and not say a word. But she loved her classes, especially those in her major—political science—and in anthropology.

"I got into it because of the past, all the different cultures," she said of anthropology. "I loved learning about all that."

The Tennessee Lady Vols huddle around Coach Pat Summitt during a game.

WELCOME TO TENNESSEE!

Summitt needed Chamique to be a scorer, and it didn't take her long to deliver. In her first college game against Virginia, Chamique had 23 points and 10 rebounds. In those days, she felt uncomfortable with the spotlight on her, and sometimes wanted to sit back and let the team's veterans take a more dominant role, even at times when she felt she could make a difference. She was very quiet, and her teammates would say, "Meek, we need you, don't fall asleep on us."

"I tried to blend in with the team," Chamique said. "I sat back and watched. I didn't know what to do. I expected the upperclassmen to lead us."

But after a 59–53 loss to Connecticut, a situation where she tried to "blend in" at the expense of the team, Chamique decided that she needed to become a more active participant in games. She told Summitt, "Next time, I'll be ready."

"I think it was just a gradual process of Chamique realizing that the team needed her to be more assertive," Summitt said. "I think she recognized that she was one of the best players on the team and she started to take that role." So Summitt was pleased when, during a game against Vanderbilt, Chamique finally grabbed her coach's jacket and said, "Coach Summitt, gimme the ball!"

Chamique was already showing flashes of the effortless grace and athleticism that she would become famous for. She could dribble behind her back, hit turnaround jumpers and post up. Her game was also showing toughness and resilience, a result of her years of playground training, back when she would bang side-by-side with the boys on the blacktop. And she had also started to earn a reputation for being levelheaded, consistent and incredibly versatile.

The honors started to roll in. Chamique became the first woman ever to be picked as ESPN's College Basketball Player of the Week. Coach Summitt declared that Chamique was the best freshman she had ever had in her program, if not the best rookie she'd ever seen.

Chamique's freshman year at Tennessee was a phenomenal success. She started in every game—an unprecedented feat for a freshman—and led the Lady Vols in scoring (16.2 points per game) and rebounding (9.1 rebounds per game) on the way to the team's fourth NCAA title. She earned several All-America honors and was the Southeastern Conference's 1996 Freshman of the Year and an All-SEC First-Team selection—the only freshman on the team.

In the SEC Tournament Final against Alabama, Chamique suffered a partial tear to the medial collateral ligament in her right knee. The injury was very frightening to her because it was the first time she had ever been hurt in her career. Chamique hated having to sit on the sidelines during practice and at games, watching her teammates play. She worked extra hard at rehab and returned 12 days later for the first

> Coach Summitt declared that Chamique was the best freshman she had ever had in her program, if not the best rookie she'd ever seen.

WELCOME TO TENNESSEE!

round of the NCAA Tournament and was able to help her team win the NCAA title.

"It's all up to me," she said. "If I'm really strong, I'll be fine. If not, it's my fault. You have to be committed, you have to do the extra work." She didn't play very hard in the first few games after her recovery because she was afraid she'd reinjure herself, but in the end she scored 88 points and grabbed 49 rebounds in the tournament and made the Final Four All-Tournament Team.

It was at the Final Four that June Holdsclaw first began to notice how much Chamique had grown. She was impressed with Chamique's development.

"I saw her play really good ball and I saw how she had stepped up her game," June said. "But I didn't tell her that because I didn't want it to go to her head."

CHAPTER 5

Not a Freshman Anymore

By the time Chamique's sophomore year began, her reputation had grown tremendously. Few teams had figured out how to defend her. She had size and quickness and could create on her shots. Her passing skills had improved, and she was already considered the best player in the women's game.

In the 1997 Midwest Regional Final, Chamique executed a 360-degree spin move off the dribble and made the basket. The move amazed onlookers, but Chamique said it was simply the result of a lot of practice—that, and the years of creative experience she had picked up from New York City playgrounds.

But it wasn't all perfect. Both Chamique and the team had some bad games and suffered through some surprising losses that season, but overall, there seemed to be more ups than downs.

Near the end of her sophomore season—in which she averaged 20.6 points and 9.4 rebounds—Chamique became the only player from Tennessee on the All-Southeastern Conference Team. She was also the only unanimous selection to *The Associated Press* All-America

Chamique and a Tennessee teammate discuss their game on the court.

First Team—and the youngest. The other four First-Teamers were all seniors.

In the postgame press conference after a Final Four semifinal in 1997, reporters asked Summitt where the Lady Vols would be without Chamique. "At home," Summitt quickly answered.

In her second Final Four, Holdsclaw was feeling much more comfortable about being in the spotlight. "I think last year I was a little overwhelmed," she said. She helped Tennessee win another NCAA title that year, marking the sixth straight time she had played on a championship team.

While Chamique was finishing up her sophomore year in college, the Women's National Basketball Association was preparing to launch its first. The WNBA would have eight teams in its first year, including one in Chamique's hometown of New York City. Another professional women's league, the American Basketball League, was already up and running.

When Chamique signed with the University of Tennessee, there had been no women's professional basketball teams in the United States. For women who wanted to play professionally, the only option was to go overseas. Both leagues, however, had rules against allowing women to leave college early to play for their teams. But that didn't stop fans and the media from wondering.

Speculation began about whether Chamique would leave school early and jump to the pros. But Chamique liked school and wanted to get her degree in political science. Besides, there was a promise she had made to her grandmother—that she would graduate.

Chamique said she realized her future was about more than just basketball. Before the women's leagues were formed, she'd thought about working for the government or going to law school. "I think what the league needs is mature young ladies who have their degrees and who want to go farther than playing basketball as a career. And I think also by playing college basketball, you develop your name. Then by your graduation or going pro, it does a greater good for the sport of women's basketball."

Chamique spent the summer of 1997 touring with USA Basketball's World Championship Qualifying team. As far she was concerned, being with the national team was like being in a classroom. She was surrounded by 11 professional basketball players who already had experience at the game's ultimate level, and she tried to learn as much as she could from veterans Teresa Edwards, Edna Campbell and Katie Smith.

Edwards was one of Chamique's favorite players and a mentor. During the team's pre-competition tour of Canada, Germany and Slovakia, the two were roommates. About halfway through the tour, Chamique heard that the roommate assignments would be switched. She immediately went to Head Coach Nell Fortner and asked if she could continue to room with Teresa. Fortner agreed, and Chamique and Teresa continued to learn from each other.

"I think they were really good for each other, the grand dame and the rookie," Fortner said. "She brought some excitement to Teresa, who in turn gave some wisdom to Chamique."

On the night of her 20th birthday, Chamique scored 32 points and led the United States to a victory over Cuba in the semifinals. Chamique finished the tour as the U.S. team's leading scorer and rebounder, while helping the squad to a 4–2 record and the silver medal. That performance earned the United States a spot in the 1998 FIBA World Championship in Berlin the following spring.

> **She became the matriarch of the Lady Vols' explosive "Three Meeks," joined by freshmen Tamika Catchings and Semeka Randall.**

In November 1997, Chamique was named USA Basketball's Female Athlete of the Year, the youngest recipient of the award since Cheryl Miller—the woman she was most often compared to—had received it in 1984.

During her third season at Tennessee, Chamique started to become the team's key leader. Both Chamique and Summitt saw the need for the superstar junior to become more vocal. Chamique also took more time to assist the team's new freshmen and be a positive role model for them.

"It all hit me last summer when I made the national team, and I was the only collegiate player," she said during her junior year. "I remember when I was in high school and wasn't even that good. Now, here I am, one of the best players in the country."

Working with the national team had raised Chamique's game to a new level. She had matured as a person and as a player and had become even more confident. The difference between her junior year and the previous season was obvious. She became the matriarch of the Lady Vols' explosive "Three Meeks," joined by freshmen Tamika Catchings and Semeka Randall.

Again, people began to wonder if Chamique would try

to leave Tennessee and join a professional league. The question came up at least twice a day. Chamique considered both sides of the issue. If she stayed in school, she would not only get a degree, but she would also have the opportunity to win four national titles at Tennessee.

But, she thought, if she left school early, she'd be able to earn a lot of money. She couldn't help but dream about being in commercials and possibly even having sneakers named after her.

But the leagues still had rules against players leaving school early, and Chamique decided she wasn't ready to leave her friends and the familiarity of college life. And she could never forget the promise to get her degree that she had made to her grandmother.

During her junior year, Chamique finally got to meet the one man she was most often compared to—Michael Jordan.

The Lady Vols visited Jordan in his office during a trip to Chicago. At first, Chamique was very shy—after all, it was Michael Jordan! After a few minutes, Chamique began to relax and was able to talk to him.

The meeting only lasted about 15 minutes, but as Chamique was preparing to leave, Jordan paid Chamique the ultimate compliment: He said he wanted to play her one-on-one!

"I was kind of shocked," Chamique said.

They didn't play each other then, but if they had, Jordan would have had his hands full. By that time in her college career, Chamique's desire to win was so strong that she wouldn't even let Summitt's young son, Tyler, win when they played video games.

THE CHAMIQUE HOLDSCLAW STORY

Chamique uses her power and height to tower over Purdue.

"I love winning," she said. "That's why we put in all the work and run all those sprints. If you're not going to get better and lay it all on the line, then why bother doing this?"

During the 1997–98 season, the University of Tennessee Lady Vols registered a remarkable accomplishment—they had the most wins and best record, a perfect 39–0, of any team, men's or women's, in NCAA basketball history.

NOT A FRESHMAN ANYMORE

The postseason ended with Chamique adding another NCAA title to her collection. After her three straight NCAA championships, Chamique had an interesting response for reporters: "I'm happy for the other players on the team. Me? I've been here before."

Her tally of consecutive championships, including those she'd won in high school, was now at seven. But Chamique wasn't concerned about any streaks. She just wanted to get better and continue to win.

In May 1998, Chamique joined the U.S. national team that would compete in the World Championship in Germany. Again, she was the only college player among a team of seasoned pros, but she still managed to score 19 points and lead a 95–89 victory over Japan in the opening game. The United States won the gold medal in the tournament.

After wrapping up the World Championship, Chamique headed to New York and began readying her game for the next step. She returned to her old bedroom in her grandmother's apartment in Queens—still plastered with all her posters, trophies and awards—and worked out four days a week at a fitness club in Manhattan to improve her strength. She also played basketball nearly every day, often playing until one A.M. She was still competing against guys, and her pickup games usually drew a crowd of people, especially children, who wanted to see the hometown hero.

CHAPTER 6

Senior Year Lessons

By the time her senior year at Tennessee began, Chamique had become a full-fledged superstar. Everywhere she went—including malls, restaurants, even the grocery store—she was asked to sign autographs. A man once asked her to sign his bare back. Even in New York City, Chamique found that she couldn't walk down the street without being stopped by fans.

The attention Chamique received was incredible. She was the star, the team's top draw. She was constantly being interviewed. Fans came from all over the country to see her and would start piling into the arena an hour and a half before tipoff. Chamique always got the loudest applause during the player introductions, and on campus other students would stare at her.

Back in New York, June would overhear conversations on the bus about Chamique. She'd listen—smiling with pride—to complete strangers reminiscing about Chamique's early years or retelling stories about Chamique's college games. "It's still strange to me that so many people know her," June said.

Chamique herself marveled at how both little boys and little girls seemed to idolize her. She saw more boys

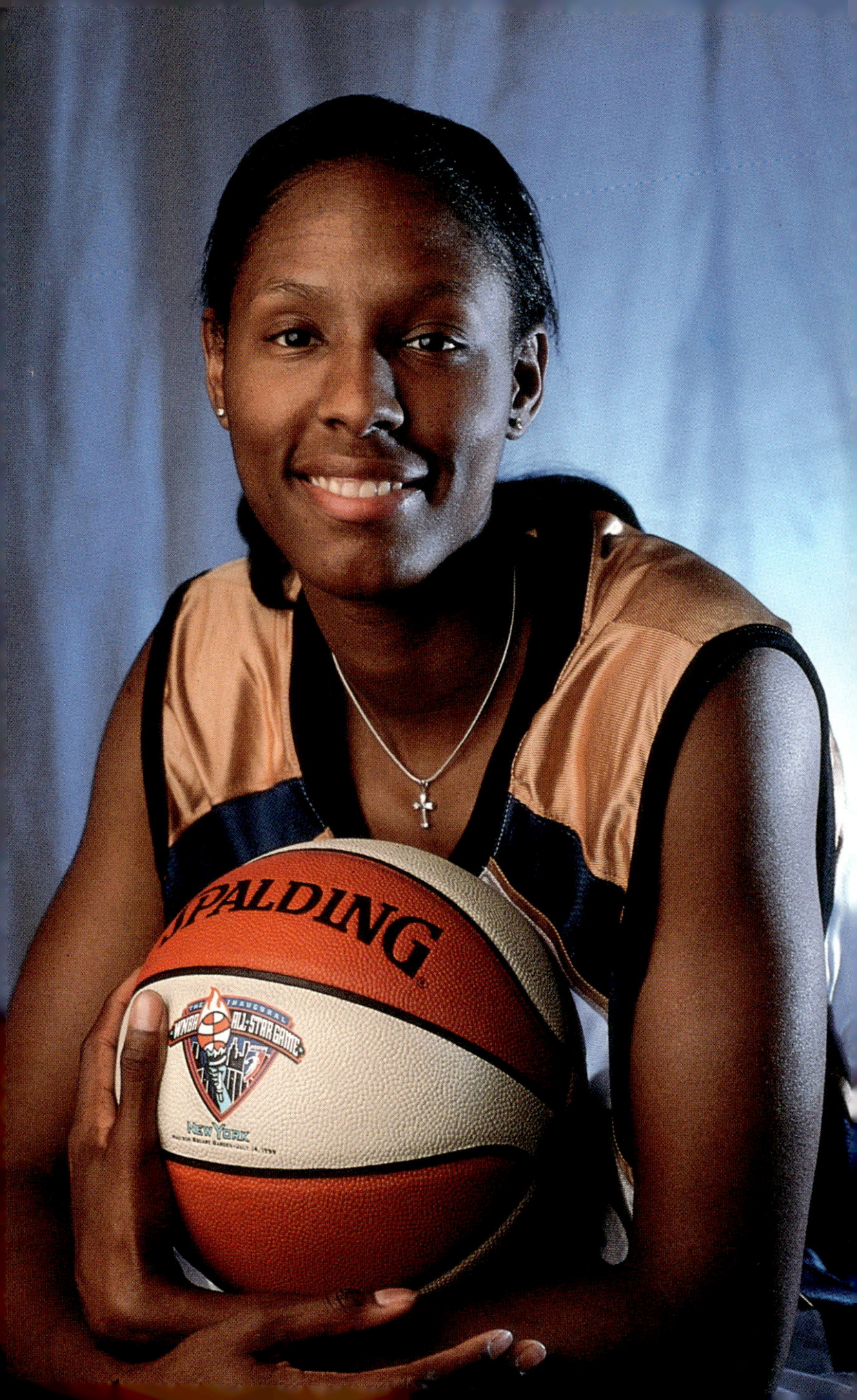
SPALDING
WNBA ALL-STAR GAME
NEW YORK

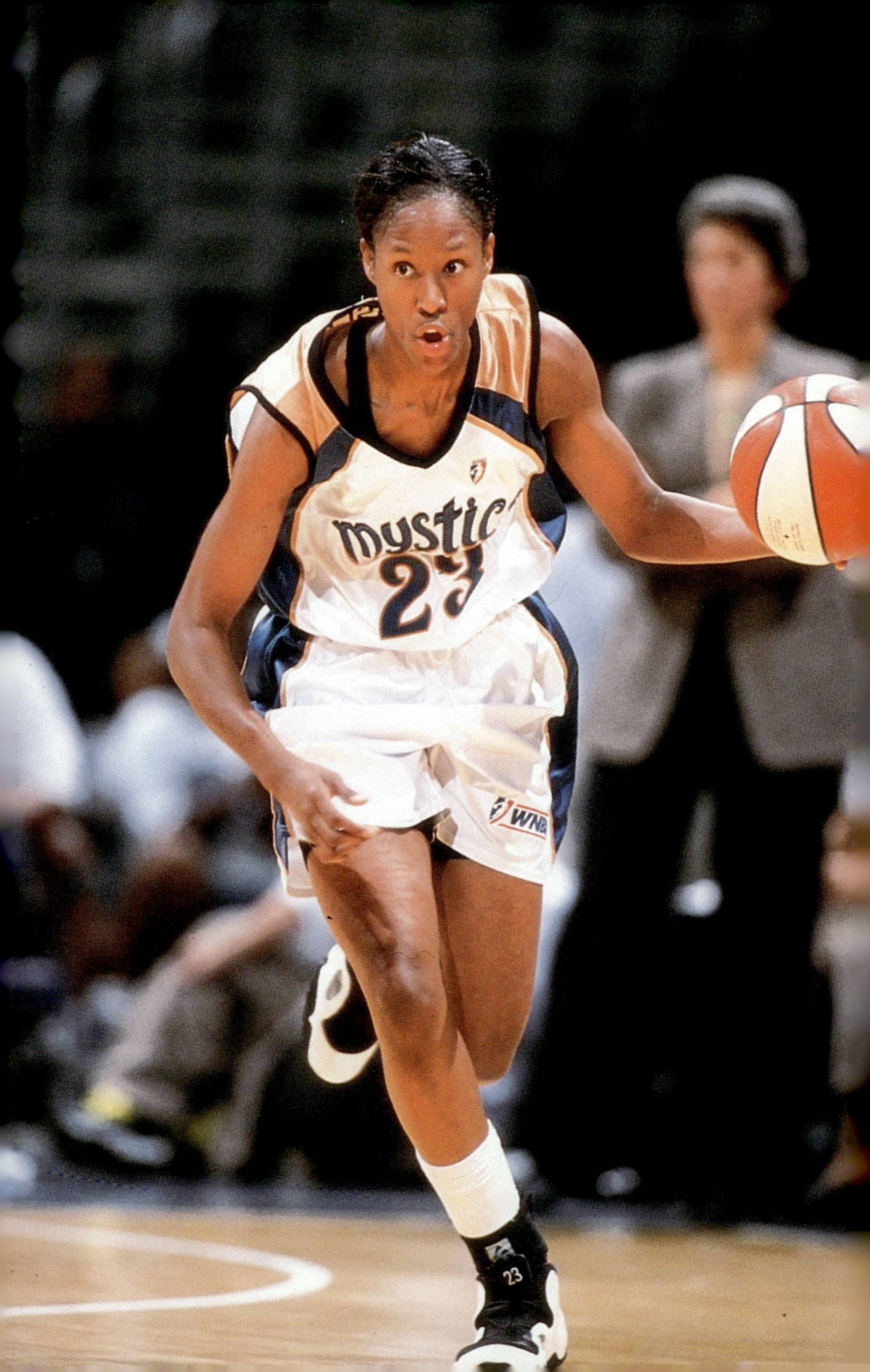
mystics
23

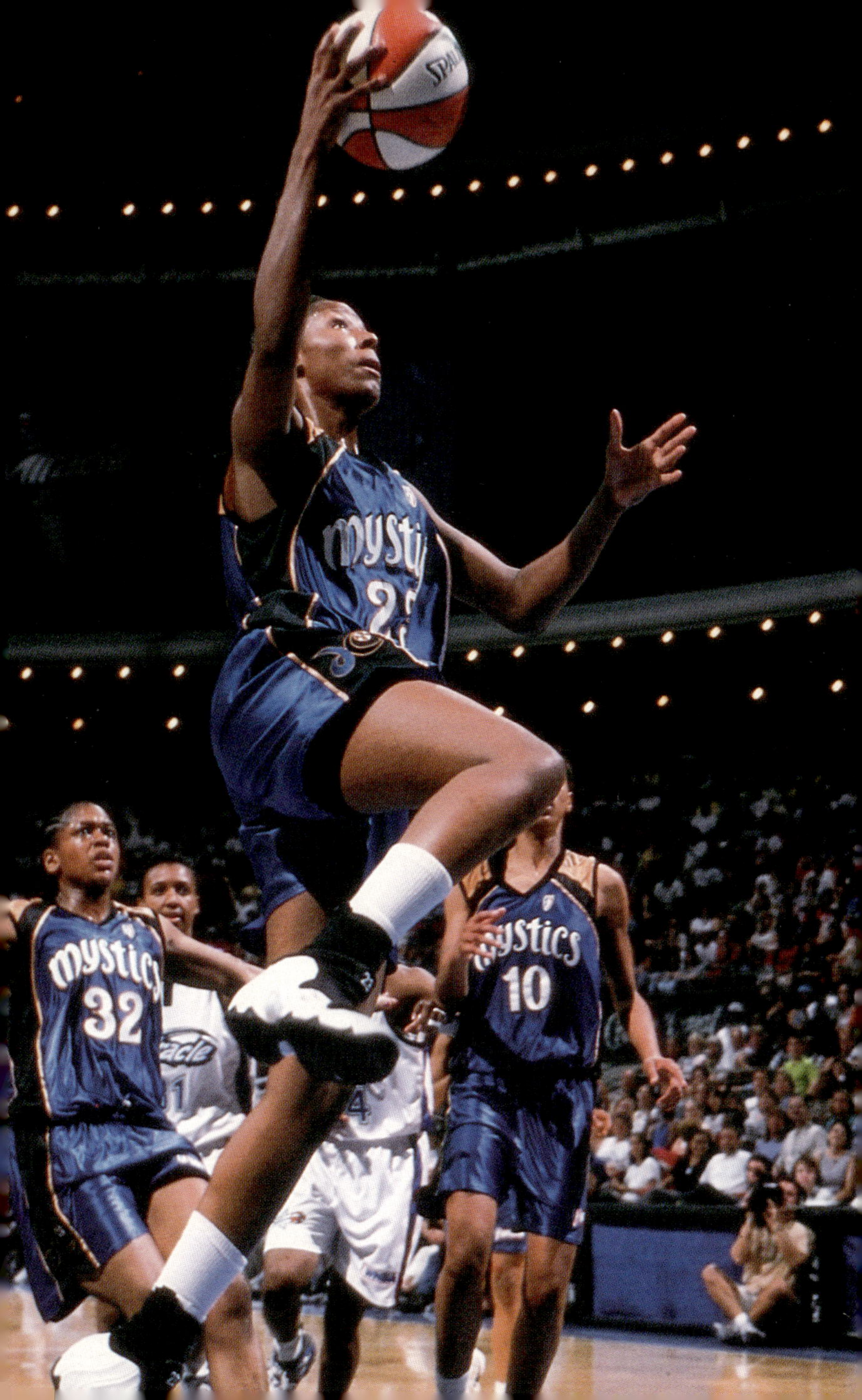
mystics
mystics
32
mystics
10

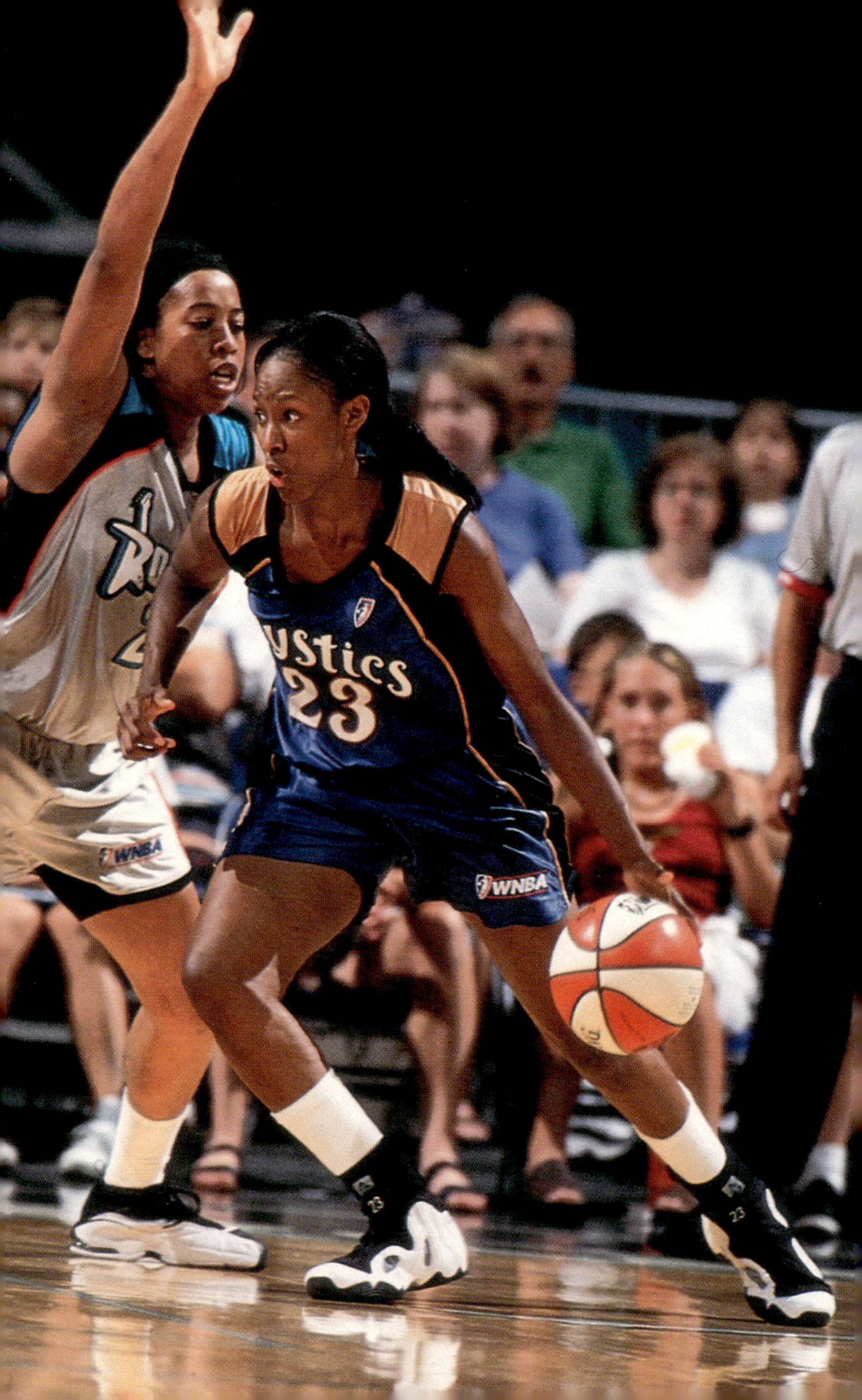
ystics
23
WNBA
WNBA

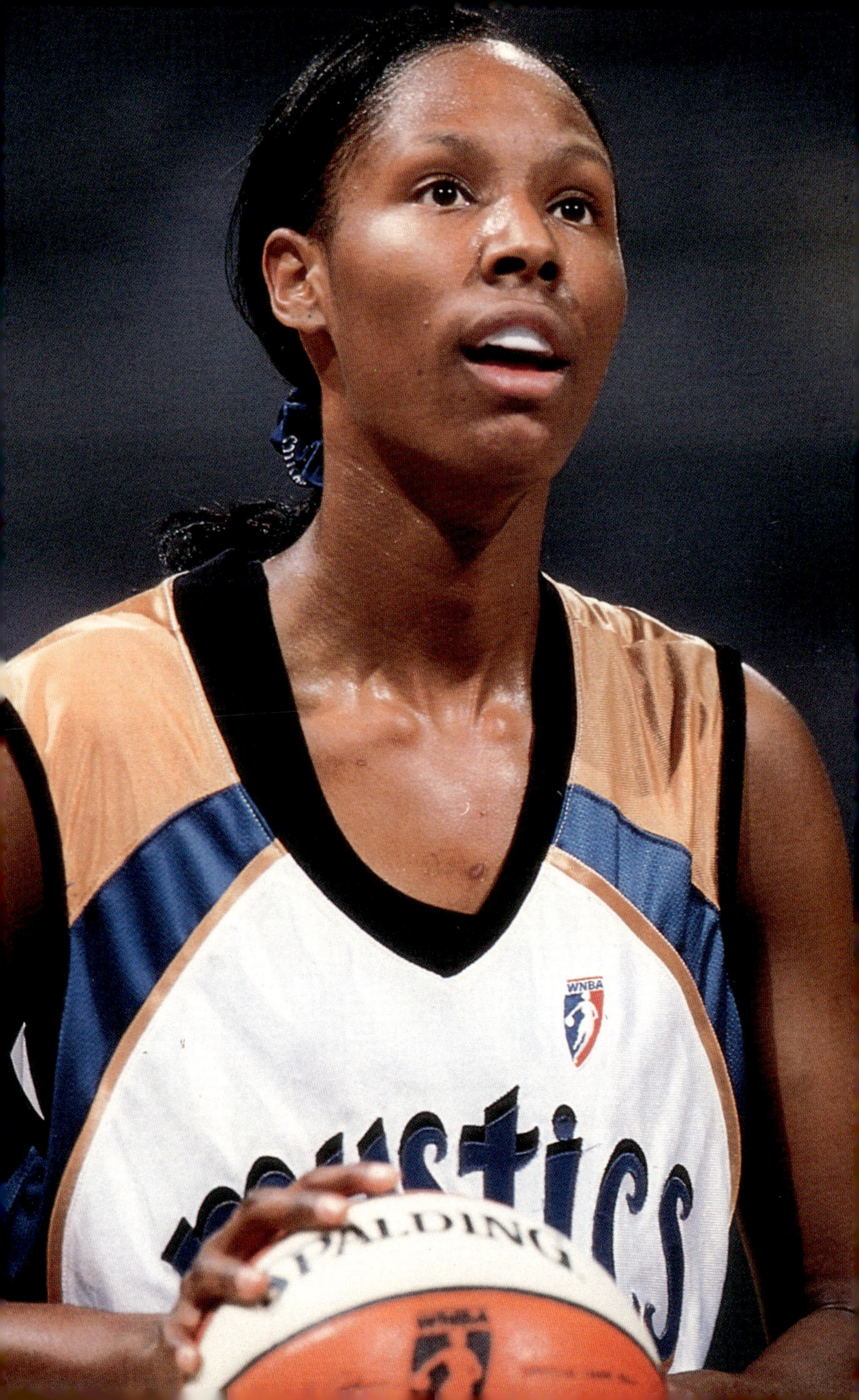
WNBA
SPALDING

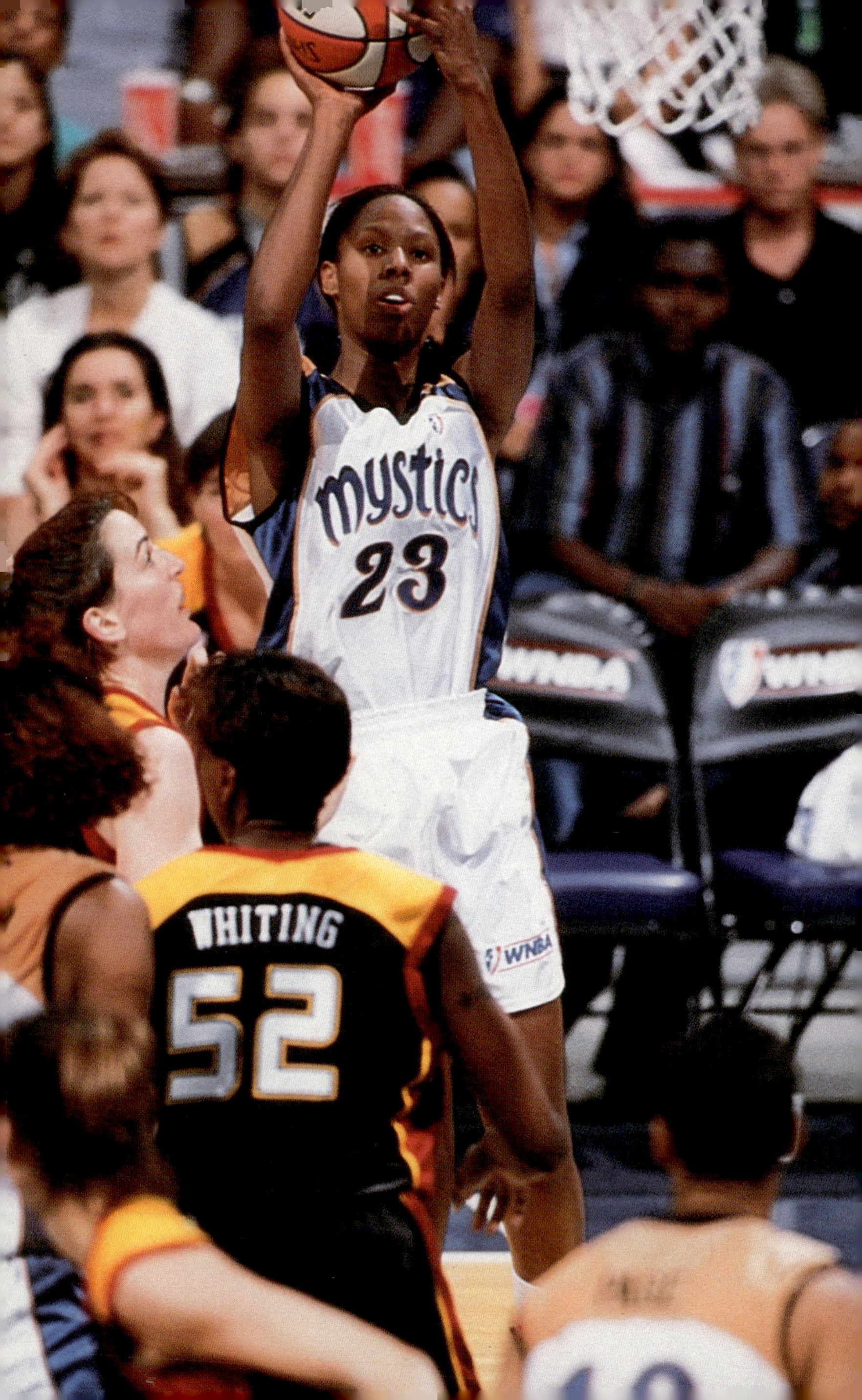
mystics
23
WHITING
52
WNBA

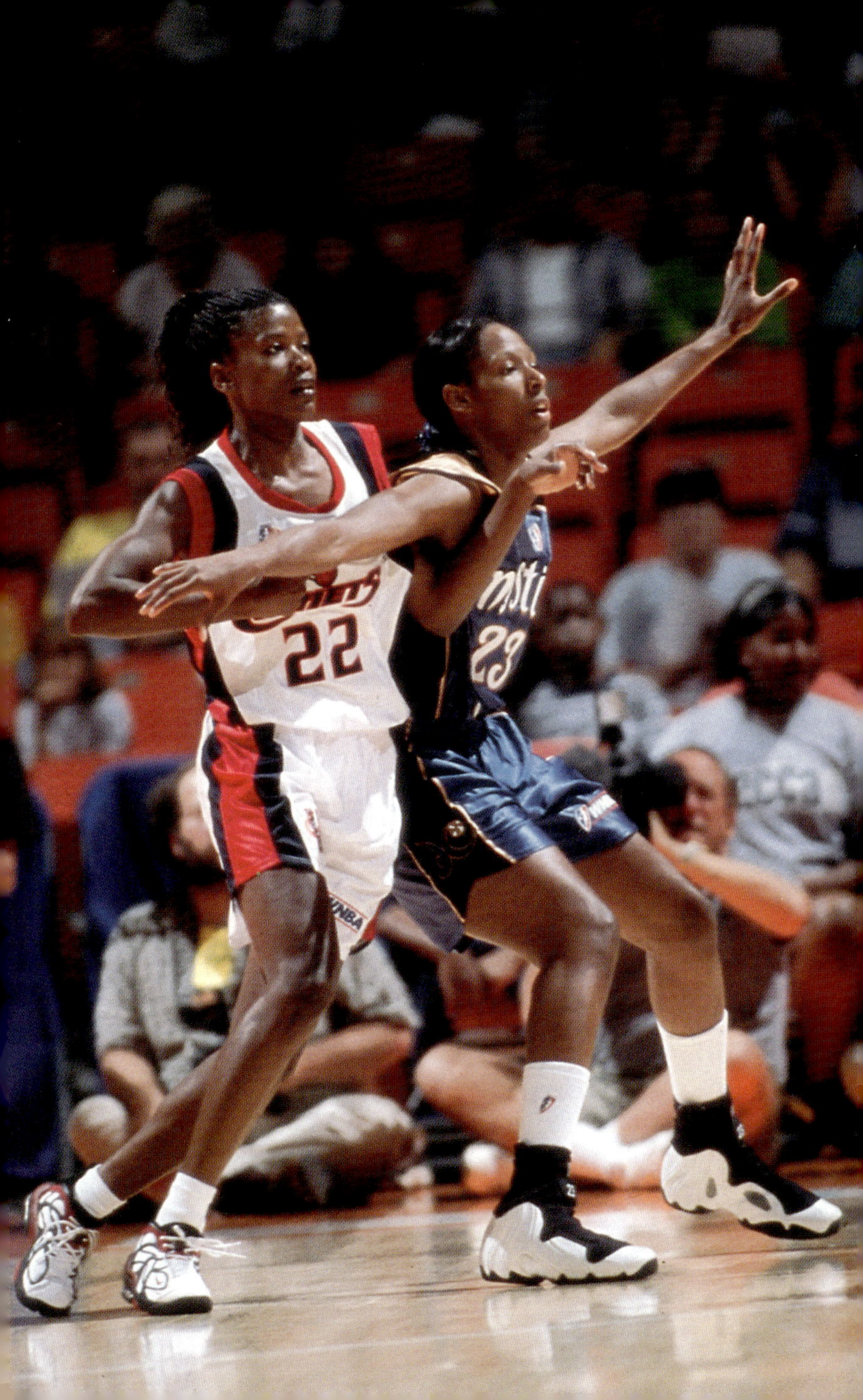
22
23

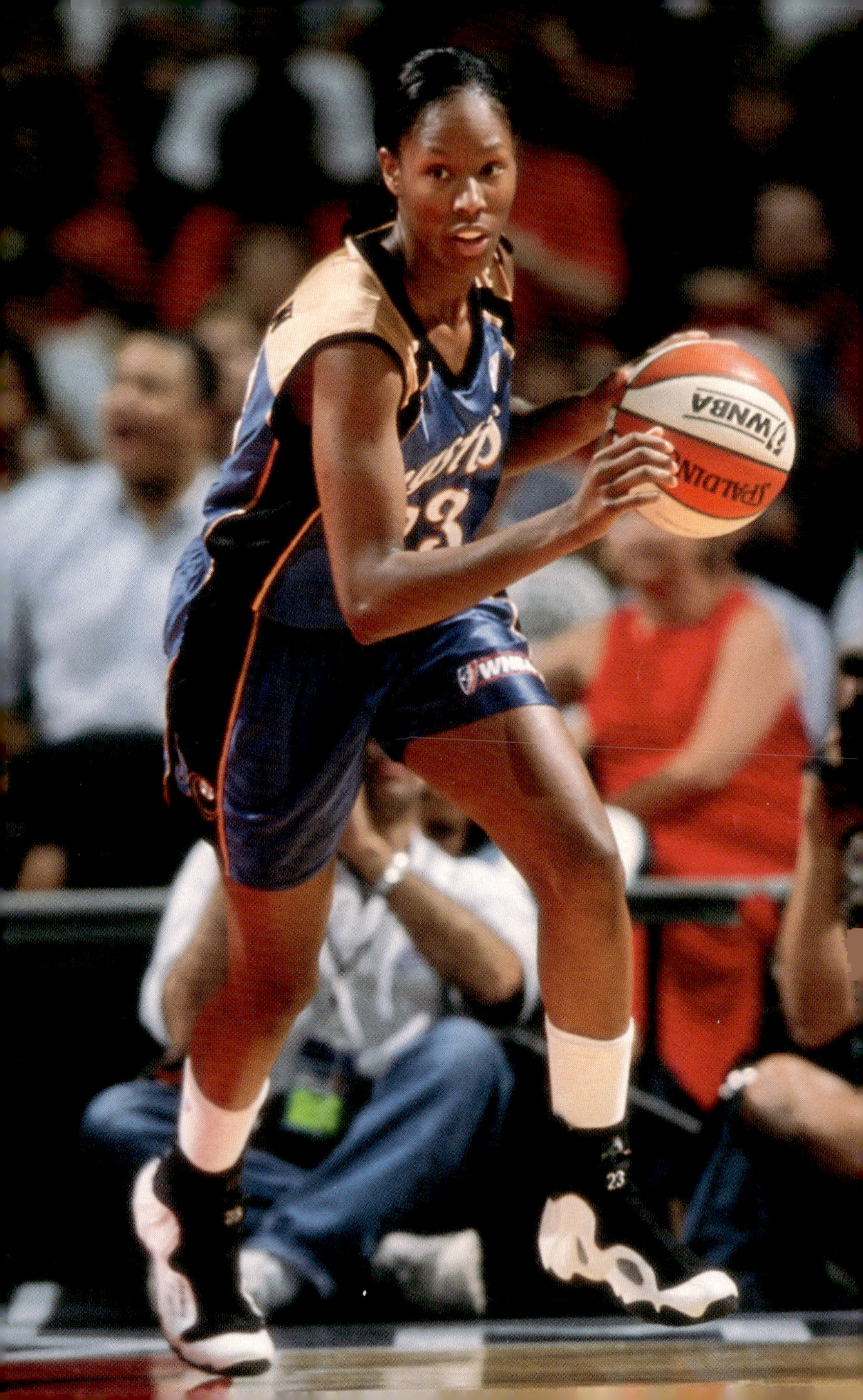
WNBA
23
WNBA

Coach Pat Summitt had faith that Chamique would become the best—she considered Chamique one of the best players to ever come through the Tennessee program.

in her jerseys than girls, and it seemed that boys asked for her autograph more often.

During the 1998–99 college season, Chamique did more than 700 interviews and photo shoots. Summitt and the women's basketball staff monitored her time carefully to keep her schedule under control. They wanted to make sure her fame didn't damage her education or interfere with her life outside of basketball.

"I think it will be a long legacy," Summitt said. "I think for years to come when you think of Tennessee, you'll think of Chamique Holdsclaw."

But Chamique remained humble and her game continued to draw more attention and more fans. Many people were attracted to her poise, confidence and self-control. Other spectators charged that she wasn't working very hard because she made it look too easy.

Chamique had returned for her senior year stronger and very serious about winning a fourth championship. She and Kellie Jolly would show up at the gym early to shoot three-pointers. Chamique was also working at being able to dunk in games.

Although newspapers and magazines gave Chamique most of the credit for the team's three NCAA titles, Chamique always wanted to give the credit to Kellie, who was the team's point guard.

"Kellie's really played an important role in every one of these championships," she explained. "Me and Kellie just play so well together. She knows where I am on the court all the time so it really helps me out as a player."

Regardless of who was responsible, the team was a hit. A sign in the Lady Vols' arena read *The Lady Vols Aren't a Team, they're a Cult*. To maintain their fantastic good luck, the team followed several game-day superstitions. Before games, each girl had to sit on her own numbered stool while Summitt discussed the game plan.

Then Chamique would lead the team through a round of chants. Sometimes, she'd yell, "I hear you knocking, but you can't come in!" At the end, the whole team would bark like dogs. Then they were ready to play ball.

Chamique was still putting a lot of work into the classroom as well. She took 12 hours the first semester of her senior year, with classes in African-American history,

American law, geriatric health and sociology.

Over the years, she had become a little more outgoing, too. Chamique said her roommate, Zakiah Modeste, had a lot to do with that. Zakiah was a track athlete at Tennessee and had grown up near New York City, in Mount Vernon, New York. "She was real outgoing, a real New York girl," Chamique said. "She really brought me out as a person."

> During the 1998–99 college season, Chamique did more than 700 interviews and photo shoots.

Throughout the season, Chamique was breaking and setting records. She set the Lady Vols' career record for rebounds, then later became the Lady Vols' all-time leading scorer. A few weeks later, she would replace former Tennessee star Allan Houston, now with the New York Knicks, as the all-time leading scorer in Tennessee basketball history. Chamique went into a game needing 18 points to break Houston's record of 2,802 points—she scored 19.

Throughout the season, Chamique continued her practice of writing messages to herself on her men's size 13 1/2 sneakers.

"They're personal motivational quotes that I need to help pump myself up, that I feel I need to be wrapped up in, and the easiest way is by my feet," she explained. She'd write whatever she was thinking about that day—if rebounding was on her mind, she'd write,

"Rebounding—believe." In her first NCAA Championship Game in 1996, she'd written "Defense Wins Championship" on her right sneaker. She also wrote "#4" on her shoes once—to support her goal to win a fourth national title.

In January 1999, Tennessee played a game at Madison Square Garden. It was the first women's collegiate basketball game played there since December 1981. The media was in a frenzy romanticizing Chamique's return to New York.

The noisy crowd of more than 15,000 that attended the game was the largest ever for a women's college basketball game at the Garden. Many people had come just to see Chamique. Summitt said that Chamique deserved the opportunity to play at the Garden in front of her devoted New York fans. Chamique only scored eight points during the game, but her fans didn't seem to be disappointed.

Chamique's incredible college career culminated in one fantastic week in February 1999. Chamique replaced Houston as Tennessee's career scoring leader (Sunday); won the Female Athlete of the Year Award (Monday); received the prestigious James E. Sullivan Memorial Award, which recognizes the nation's top amateur athlete (Thursday); and was honored at her last regular-season home game (Thursday night).

The Sullivan award was probably the most notable highlight of the week. Chamique was the first female basketball player—and only the third basketball player ever—to win the award in its 69-year history. Among basketball players, she followed Bill Walton, who won

SENIOR YEAR LESSONS

By her senior season, Chamique had won three NCAA Championships and her opponents knew they had to get by her for a victory.

THE CHAMIQUE HOLDSCLAW STORY

the award in 1973, and Bill Bradley, who won in 1965.

Sullivan honorees are chosen for demonstrating leadership, character and sportsmanship. Chamique's competition included Elton Brand, now a member of the Chicago Bulls, and Heisman Trophy winner Ricky Williams, now a running back for the New Orleans Saints.

Chamique's season had gone so well that it looked like she and teammate Kellie Jolly would become the first players to win four national titles at the collegiate level. At the NCAA East Regional Finals Chamique often carried around a video camera to capture behind-the-scenes looks of what she hoped would be another NCAA win and the end of a perfect collegiate career.

But she wasn't trying to put pressure on herself, and neither was the team.

"She is at the top of the list as far having the single greatest impact on our game to date," Summitt said then. "I don't think if Chamique falls short of four championships it will lessen what she has already done here."

In the first games of the NCAA Tournament, Chamique put up exceptional numbers. She tied her career high with 39 points in Tennessee's second-round game. But Chamique's last game as a Lady Vol, the 1999 East Regional Final against Duke, was one of the worst of her career.

GIRL POWER!
In her senior year of college, Chamique broke Allan Houston's record as all-time leading scorer in Tennessee basketball history.

SENIOR YEAR LESSONS

Duke ended Tennessee's three-year run as national champions with a 69–63 victory. Chamique missed her first 10 shots and finished 2-for-18 from the field for eight points—matching her season low. She hit only 4-of-8 free throws and committed five turnovers.

Chamique fouled out of the game with 25.4 seconds left and received a standing ovation. She broke down in tears as she returned to the bench. It was the first time she had failed to win a championship since junior high school.

"I think it's obvious we're in pain," Summitt said in post-game interviews. "Our seniors are champions. Three out of four is not bad."

June Holdsclaw was there to comfort her granddaughter. She felt badly for Chamique, but wanted her to understand that she was still a champion.

"Chamique, you have been blessed all through elementary school, high school and now college," she told her. "You have won three championships. Even in the AAU, you have always been like a champ. This is not the worst thing in life. You haven't had any terrible injuries or anything—you have been blessed."

June said losing the tournament was a great experience for Chamique because she had experienced disappointment and would have to learn to deal with it. Summitt agreed that Chamique learned much more from her final college loss than from the three titles that preceded it.

"It's good for her to understand that you don't always win," Summitt said. For her part, Chamique said she never felt that she was invincible, but was devastated nonetheless. The loss put a new determination in her heart. She realized that as soon as her college season ended, her new life would begin.

"Just like you handle winning, you have to handle failure," Chamique said.

"You know, [most] people don't even win conference championships," she explained. "They are happy just to win that. I'm so lucky to go out and win three national championships."

After her last game at the University of Tennessee's Thompson-Boling Arena, Chamique kissed the floor and waved good-bye to Lady Vol fans. But after four years of remarkable achievements, they wouldn't forget Chamique—they couldn't. A few weeks later, the city of Knoxville named a street near the arena after her.

"She's an amazing young woman and we're proud she played for our Lady Vols and lived in Knoxville," said Knoxville mayor Victor Ashe. "I believe we are a better community today because Chamique lived here and played at the University of Tennessee."

Although she still had to face graduation and the WNBA draft, Chamique knew that her life would be changing dramatically. During all of the excitement of her senior year, Chamique called Hall of Famer Cheryl Miller for advice.

"People have compared me to her a lot, so I wanted to talk to her," Chamique said. "At first she didn't believe it was me. I had to convince her, but we had a good conversation."

Miller told Chamique not to lose sight of what it takes to be the best and reminded her that no matter how great a player she is, there's always room for improvement.

"But more importantly," Miller said, "handle everything with a grain of salt and don't ever think that you or one player is bigger than the team or the game."

There was a lot of talk about whether Chamique would join the WNBA's New York Liberty and play in front of her New York fans. The rumors had grown more persistent after she was spotted a few times in the crowd during Liberty games at Madison Square Garden. Chamique liked the idea of being able to play before family and friends, but because the WNBA does not allow regional draft picks, Chamique had to go through the draft like everyone else. The Washington Mystics, not the New York Liberty, had the first pick in the 1999 WNBA Draft, and there was little doubt that Chamique would be No. 1.

CHAPTER 7

Welcome to the WNBA

Few people were surprised when on May 4, 1999, WNBA President Val Ackerman walked up to a podium at the WNBA Draft in New York City and announced the first selection.

"With the first pick of the 1999 WNBA Draft, the Washington Mystics have selected Chamique Holdsclaw from the University of Tennessee," Ackerman announced with a smile.

As Chamique stood on the stage holding a Washington Mystics jersey and posing for photographs, she couldn't help but reflect on how far she had come in her career.

"I was so excited," she said. "I was like, 'Thank you, Lord, this is such a blessing.'"

Chamique was eager to go to Washington, and was looking forward to the outstanding fan support the Mystics boasted. She was also excited about playing for Mystics Coach Nancy Darsch, who had been endorsed by Tennessee Coach Pat Summitt.

Summitt also had a prediction for the Mystics' 1999 season: "I'll tell you this," Summitt said to *The Washington Post*. "Washington will definitely win more

Chamique greets a Mystics teammate during her first season in the WNBA.

THE CHAMIQUE HOLDSCLAW STORY

Chamique dazzles her opponents with moves she picked up on New York City playgrounds.

WELCOME TO THE WNBA

than three games."

Although the stage would be a little different, some things had not changed. Chamique was determined to win, and she thought that she could make a significant contribution to the Mystics.

"I'm going to win," she said. "So I'm willing to sacrifice my own game. If I can just bring that winning attitude every day to the table, I think I'm going to be all right, I know my team's going to be okay."

> **Chamique's debut with the Mystics was one of the most eagerly anticipated events of the season.**

Chamique's debut with the Mystics was one of the most eagerly anticipated events of the season. Many people considered her the player who would carry the women's game into the next century. That might have been a heavy responsibility for anyone else, but Chamique took it all in stride.

"I think I feel a sense of responsibility for the game, but to put it on one person's shoulders I guess is unfair because I feel there's a lot of great players and a lot of players who are capable of carrying the torch," she said. "I can only do what I'm comfortable doing and what I'm capable of doing."

Mystics Coach Nancy Darsch knew that high expectations were being put on Chamique. Darsch asked fans to be patient, and not to expect miracles.

"Any time a player jumps to the next level, there's

going to be an adjustment period, a transition period," Darsch said. "Chamique has a great future ahead of her, and we're going to have to take some time and assimilate her into the team, the system, the new experiences, the demands of travel and the schedule of the WNBA. She definitely has a very, very bright future. She is and will be a great player. It just might not be every day at this point."

> "When I graduated, it was the greatest day of my life just to see the excitement on my grandma's face."

Everyone wanted to watch Chamique play, but they had to wait a little bit longer—she missed the first two days of training camp because of her graduation from Tennessee and Kellie Jolly's wedding. Chamique's college graduation was a big event—for her and for her family. June Holdsclaw was so excited to see her first grandchild graduate from college that she almost fainted.

"My grandmother said, 'You promised me that you're going to graduate in four years and stay in school and do it,'" Chamique remembered. "And when I graduated, it was the greatest day of my life just to see the excitement on my grandma's face."

When she arrived at the Mystics' training camp, Chamique found that she faced a small problem: Jersey No. 23 was already taken. Chamique's teammate on the Mystics, Rita Williams, had worn No. 23 in the 1998 WNBA season. So after years of winning with 23 on her

WELCOME TO THE WNBA

back, Chamique now faced the possibility of having to start over with a new number.

But the dilemma didn't last long. Rita made a deal with Chamique two days into training camp that gave Chamique the right to wear Mystics No. 23. In exchange, Chamique agreed to buy Rita golf clubs so that the two could take lessons together. "She told me I had to pay for her lessons, too," Chamique said.

With her new jersey in hand, Chamique was now ready for her pro debut.

CHAPTER 8

Let the Games Begin!

In her first WNBA preseason game, Chamique was a little nervous. She wasn't sure if she should do the same things that she had done at Tennessee, and she wanted to be sure she wasn't a "ball hog."

But all her nervousness didn't really seem to matter, especially to the crowd that came out to watch the Mystics at Washington's MCI Center. Chamique grabbed the first rebound of the game, then scored her first points on a short turnaround baseline jumper less than five minutes into the game. She punctuated her first two points with a huge smile. Everything Chamique did that evening brought cheers from the crowd, and even her airballs were greeted warmly. She finished the game with 14 points, 13 rebounds and a win for the Mystics.

Another preseason game was held at Chamique's alma mater, the University of Tennessee. The Mystics played the Houston Comets in the game that was held in conjunction with the opening of the Women's Basketball Hall of Fame in Knoxville. Although the Comets were the reigning WNBA champs, Chamique and her Mystics teammate Nikki McCray—also a former Tennessee star—were the centers of attention. For Chamique, the event

Mystics' jersey number 23 was taken when Chamique arrived at training camp, but Chamique convinced teammate Rita Williams to give it up. Chamique grew up wearing number 23.

was a fitting way to say good-bye to Tennessee basketball fans one last time.

Chamique scored 20 points and had 10 rebounds and six assists in the Mystics' 68–64 victory over Houston, and it seemed that perhaps another fairy-tale season was under way.

June Holdsclaw, who was sitting in the audience at the Knoxville game, felt tingles when Chamique's name was announced. The atmosphere was positively electric for the proud grandmother.

On the day of her first regular-season WNBA game, June 10, 1999, Chamique appeared on *Good Morning America*. She expected to feel chills down her spine when she heard her name announced for the first time as a pro. She did.

The Mystics hosted the Charlotte Sting at the MCI Center before a sellout crowd of 20,674. Chamique's family had taken the train from New York to see her debut, and the audience was filled with notable faces, including several players from the NBA's Washington Wizards.

Chamique scored 18 points and grabbed six rebounds, but the Mystics lost the game 83–73. That was another first for Chamique: She had never lost a season opener. She didn't like it. "I can't get used to it," she told reporters after the game. "We just have to work harder."

Chamique's life in the WNBA became even more hectic than it had been at Tennessee. Her schedule was constantly booked with public appearances, practices and games. If she had any spare time, she would go to amusement parks, to the movies, or hang out with the few people she knew in the Washington, D.C., area. She found that her fame made it a little tough to make friends.

"I've met some good people, but I really don't have that many friends," she said. "My grandmother always told me, 'If you have one, that's good enough.' I meet people, but it's hard today to realize who's your friend for the right reasons."

As Chamique began to make more money from her WNBA contract and endorsements, she put herself on a budget and was careful about what she spent her money on. She didn't want to get carried away. She bought a sport-utility vehicle and rented a townhouse in Alexandria, Virginia, where she planned to live year-round. Chamique said she didn't want to live in New York because there were too many "distractions." She meant that there were too many people in New York who might have expected too many things from her, like tickets, money and some of the trappings from her fame. It would have been difficult to say no.

> **She expected to feel chills down her spine when she heard her name announced for the first time as a pro. She did.**

"You know, they always say that it [fame] changes you," she said. "But you don't change, your friends do."

Chamique performed well in the first few weeks of the 1999 season, and at the end of June she was named the WNBA Player of the Week. In that period, she averaged 21.5 points, 11.5 rebounds and 5.5 assists. But Mystics fans soon found out that adding Chamique to the roster did not prove to be the miracle cure for the team. The team got off to a rocky start and struggled for wins. For the first time in her life, Chamique knew what it felt like to be on a losing team.

"At first it was hard, but I realized I'm going to have to go through some growing pains," Chamique said. "I've been spoiled. I guess I've always enjoyed a lot of success, but losing that championship in college was probably the best thing for me. Right now I'm disappointed, but I know it's going to get better and I know that this team is going to be a championship-caliber team."

The media started to wonder if Chamique had been hyped up a little too much, or if the pros were too much for her to handle. There was also talk that other players in the league were getting tired of the Chamique hype. Despite all the attention she received—good and bad—Chamique insisted she did not feel pressured. She continued to maintain a double-digit scoring average and, although she wasn't perfect, did the best she could to help the team.

"I knew what I was capable of doing," she said. "It's just a matter of staying focused. There's a lot of good players out there, but I think that what takes you to another level is that mental toughness, and even if I'm not on top of my game, I know I'm tough mentally, and I'm going to do what my team needs me to do. The sky's the limit. I know I'm a pretty good player. One thing I'm going to do is get better."

Chamique's coach and teammates also had a lot of faith in her future. "She can pretty much do it all,"

LET THE GAMES BEGIN!

Darsch said. "I think she shows the kind of potential ...[to] be one of the best."

Nikki McCray, who had been the Mystics' headliner in its first season, agreed that Chamique still had some growing to do. "I think she will become a phenomenal player," she said. "And I think that's going to take time."

Through it all, Chamique maintained her positive outlook. She went after every game as if she had not lost the last one. She would tell her teammates, "We're not going to lose this game. There's no way we're going to lose this game," to pep them up before they hit the court.

"Just to hear that from a rookie, it makes you want to

Chamique and Nikki McCray, two of Washington's star players and former Lady Vols, lead the Mystics during a game.

step up and play harder," said teammate Murriel Page.

At midseason, the WNBA held its first-ever WNBA All-Star Game. For weeks before the game, fans were able to cast their votes for their favorite WNBA players. From the beginning, Chamique was one of the fans' favorites—although she didn't keep track of how her votes compared to other players.

When the returns came in, Chamique—who had played less than 15 games in her pro career—led all Eastern Conference players in votes received with 62,841 votes. And she was the only rookie to make the All-Star roster.

The inaugural WNBA All-Star Game was held at Madison Square Garden in New York on July 14, 1999. For days leading up to the game, Chamique seemed to be the center of attention. Back in her hometown, she was still a hero. She was mobbed by autograph seekers at the NBA Store and circled by reporters at WNBA press conferences. Through it all, Chamique said the attention did not faze her. "I'm just focused on this team, just trying to win," she said. "I'm used to winning. All this individual stuff comes second to me."

The game was an exciting, star-studded affair. Five

> **A LAWYER ON THE COURT?**
> If the WNBA hadn't offered her a chance to play basketball professionally, Chamique would possibly have taken her political science major to law school.

LET THE GAMES BEGIN!

members of the World Cup champion U.S. women's soccer team were in the audience, as were celebrities Tyra Banks, Gregory Hines, Spike Lee, Queen Latifah, Joan Jett and Liza Minnelli. Whitney Houston, one of Chamique's favorite singers, sang the national anthem. Chamique got some of the loudest applause during the introductions.

But the unexpected happened just minutes into the game, when Chamique took a pass from Teresa Weatherspoon, and Michele Timms, who was defending against Chamique, tried to steal the ball. "The ball just hit me dead on the tip of the finger," Chamique said. She had to leave the game, and X rays later showed that she had suffered a chip fracture in her left index finger. It was expected that the broken finger would keep her sidelined for as long as three weeks.

"But I think I'll be playing this Saturday," Chamique told reporters.

Although Chamique was disappointed about missing most of her first All-Star Game, she still enjoyed the experience, even though the West beat her Eastern Conference team, 79–61. "I was playing well, I was excited and our team was coming back," she said. "It was fun though. I got to hang around a lot of great players, be a part of history. What else could I ask for?"

Although doctors had expected Chamique to miss several games because of her finger injury, Chamique lived up to her prediction and was indeed playing the following Saturday, in a road game against the Charlotte Sting.

Chamique played with a metal brace on her finger, and seemed to have no problems dribbling or passing. Even so, the Mystics lost to the Sting, 63–56.

THE CHAMIQUE HOLDSCLAW STORY

Chamique works on her outside shot at practice. She is on her way to becoming one of the best players in the WNBA.

LET THE GAMES BEGIN!

"You can't be a baby in this league," she explained about coming back early from the injury. "I get paid to play. It'll be sore, but it'll also be sore three weeks from now."

In the weeks following the All-Star Game, the Mystics struggled to improve and to earn a spot in the WNBA playoffs. The team set off on a 12-day, six-game West Coast road trip. It was on that trip, Chamique said, that the players got to know one another a little better. Their new closeness began to show in their performances.

"Just being around each other, getting more unity, learning each other a little bit better," Chamique said. "It just has let us play with a little more heart and more passion because we're playing together as a team and we trust each other a little bit more."

The Mystics lost four consecutive games on that trip, but they finally snapped their losing streak by defeating the Detroit Shock at The Palace of Auburn Hills. Chamique finished with 23 points and had seven rebounds and five assists.

"One of the things Coach put on the board before the game tonight was, 'Play with a lot of heart,'" Holdsclaw said. "I think we did that. At the end of a road trip like this, you get down mentally, but we haven't done that. We're still trying to have fun."

The Mystics were now on a hot streak and Chamique earned another Player of the Week Award for the first week of August—when she led the Mystics to a 4–0 record, averaging 22 points and shooting .571 from the field.

On the night before her 22nd birthday, Chamique

helped the Mystics in an 80–45 win over the Cleveland Rockers. A move by Chamique made the highlight reel: With 20 seconds left in the first half, Chamique cut to the basket, jumped and twisted to catch a pass from Nikki McCray. She caught the ball in midair, and in one smooth move turned and made the 10-foot basket.

> "I don't care about the individual thing," she would say. "I came here to try to make this organization a championship team."

The victory was the Mystics' fourth straight win, and it brought the team to within three games of the playoffs with only five games left. And to top it all off, the crowd of 15,512 fans at the MCI Center sang "Happy Birthday" to Chamique.

After the game, players danced on the court and couldn't hide their excitement. The Mystics locker room was like a house party. "I'm not going to sit here and say that we're going to make the playoffs," said Chamique, who scored 18 points in that game. "But we're going to keep fighting, and we're going to do our best trying."

From that point on, Chamique said everything seemed to be wide open. The team was playing better defense and showing more passion.

"Hopefully, even if we don't make the playoffs, we know that we've created something special," Chamique said. "We know what it takes for this team to go out there and win. We just have to continue doing that. If we don't make it, there's next year, and we just come in here with the same attitude that we have displayed in these last couple of games."

The possibility of making it into the playoffs gave Chamique and the team more of a boost than they would have expected. Even with everything they'd gone through during the season, the Mystics were not feeling the exhaustion that players usually feel at season's end.

"I feel like I'm in the best shape of my life," Chamique said. "It's crunch time, and at crunch time is when the real champions come to the table. I can't be thinking I'm tired now. I know that my team needs me and I have to go out there and try to perform."

Meanwhile, Chamique was constantly being asked how she would feel to be Rookie of the Year. She always said that it would be great to win the award, but that she was more focused on her team. "I don't care about the individual thing," she would say. "I came here to try to make this organization a championship team."

For a while, it looked as if the Mystics would be the rags-to-riches story of the 1999 WNBA season. After scoring their fifth straight victory with a win over the New York Liberty, Washington was only two games out of the third and final playoff spot in the East. The Mystics' sixth straight win—a franchise record—came just a few days later against the Los Angeles Sparks. The team, Chamique said, was playing with heart.

"It's a blessing that the season's ending up this way," Chamique said. "Our destiny's in our own hands, and that's pressure, but it's a good pressure."

> **DINNER DATE**
> Who in history would Chamique most like to have dinner with? Not a movie star or a singer, but with the great civil rights leader, Dr. Martin Luther King, Jr.

Unfortunately, the team's exciting ride soon ended with an 81–54 loss to the Orlando Miracle. The loss eliminated Washington from WNBA playoff contention.

Not making it to the playoffs was disappointing for Chamique, but she had won in many other ways. At the end of her first WNBA season, Chamique received 48 of 51 votes from a panel of sportswriters and broadcasters to win the 1999 WNBA Rookie of the Year Award.

Chamique was able to look back on her debut season and talk about the pressure that had been placed on her to be the face and name of the women's game. She thought she'd handled everything just fine. Her goal, she said, had been to "go out there and try to win games and just play basketball."

"That's what my focus is," she said. "It's not on what I'm supposed to be promoting and who I'm supposed to be doing this for. It's just about being comfortable with myself and comfortable with this team and realizing what I'm here for—and that's to play basketball and be who I am, not to please everybody."

Even though her first season in the WNBA wasn't the stuff fairy tales are made of, Chamique believes a WNBA championship is still waiting for her down the road. In the end, Chamique helped the Mystics win four times as

LET THE GAMES BEGIN!

many games in 1999 as they had in 1998.

"This team is the youngest team in the WNBA, we have a lot of talent, we're only going to get better," said Chamique. "In two years, this team is going to be one to be reckoned with because we have all the elements.

"I think, once you believe what you can do, the sky's the limit."

CAREER HIGHLIGHTS

HIGH SCHOOL

★ Led Christ the King High School to four consecutive state championships and one national title, with an overall record of 106–4

★ Named the New York state MVP in 1993, 1994 and 1995

★ Named New York City's Player of the Year for three consecutive years, the first player to do so

COLLEGE

★ Tennessee's all-time leading scorer (3,025) and rebounder (1,295)

★ First woman ever to be chosen as ESPN's College Basketball Player of the Week

★ Was the fifth player in NCAA women's basketball history to reach 3,000 career points

CAREER HIGHLIGHTS

★ First women's collegiate basketball player to win the James E. Sullivan Memorial Award, which recognizes the nation's top amateur athlete

INTERNATIONAL

★ Named USA Basketball's Female Athlete of the Year in 1997

★ Received a gold medal at the 1998 World Championship

★ Named to the 1999–2000 USA Basketball Women's National Team

WNBA

★ Was voted a starter for the Eastern Conference team for the inaugural WNBA All-Star Game, played on July 14, 1999

★ Named the 1999 WNBA Rookie of the Year